YA 658.834 Wit
Wittekind, Erika, 1980-
The big push : how popular
culture
is always selling /

34028080339899
**CYF** $8.95    ocn754105646
                 08/06/12

**W9-BGU-959**

3  4028  08033  9899
HARRIS COUNTY PUBLIC LIBRARY

2012

# THE BIG PUSH

## HOW POPULAR CULTURE IS ALWAYS SELLING

by Erika Wittekind

**Content Consultant:** John V. Pavlik,
Professor and Chair, Department of Journalism and Media Studies,
School of Communication and Information, Rutgers University

COMPASS POINT BOOKS
a capstone imprint

EXPLORING
MEDIA LITERACY

Compass Point Books
1710 Roe Crest Drive
North Mankato, MN 56003

Copyright © 2012 by Compass Point Books, a Capstone imprint.
All rights reserved. No part of this book may be reproduced without written
permission from the publisher. The publisher takes no responsibility for the use of any
of the materials or methods described in this book, nor for the products thereof.

Editors: Mari Kesselring and Lauren Coss
Designers: Becky Daum and Kazuko Collins

Image Credits
Fernando Alonso Herrero/iStockphoto, cover; Helga Esteb/Shutterstock Images,
back cover (left); Luca di Filippo/iStockphoto, back cover (center); Adam J. Sablich/
Shutterstock Images, back cover (right); Ronald Martinez/Getty Images, 5; Richard
Levine/Alamy, 6; Red Line Editorial, 7, 27, 51, 59; Alex J. Berliner/AP Images, 8;
Shutterstock Images, 13, 14, 31, 53, 67; Fox Searchlight/Photofest, 17; Chris Pizzello/
AP Images, 19; Candy Box Images/Shutterstock Images, 21; Old Paper Studios/
Alamy, 22; Jeff Morgan 13/Alamy, 24; David Kilpatrick/Alamy, 28; Daniel Deitschel/
iStockphoto, 30; Daniel Laflor/iStockphoto, 32; Nuno Garuti/Bigstock, 35; Robert
Landau/Alamy, 36; PR Newswire/AP Images, 38; James Brey/iStockphoto, 41;
Margot Petrowski/iStockphoto, 43; Tischenko Irina/Shutterstock Images, 45; Andres
Rodriguez/Bigstock, 46; iStockphoto, 47, 56, 73, 75; Andrew Kent/Getty Images, 50;
Felipe Dana/AP Images, 52; Sara Gray/iStockphoto, 55; Fox Broadcasting/Photofest,
58; Eugene Gurevich/Bigstock, 61; AP Images, 62; Daniel Boczarski/Getty Images, 65;
Kathy Dewar/iStockphoto, 70; Irourii Tcheka/ Shutterstock Images, 71; Edward Bock/
iStockphoto, 72

Design elements: Becky Daum/Red Line Editorial

This book was manufactured with paper containing at least
10 percent post-consumer waste.

Library of Congress Cataloging-in-Publication Data
Wittekind, Erika, 1980–
  The big push : how popular culture is always selling / by Erika Wittekind.
    p. cm.— Exploring media literacy)
  Includes bibliographical references and index.
  ISBN 978-0-7565-4518-5 (library binding)
  ISBN 978-0-7565-4535-2 (paperback)
  1. Consumer behavior—Juvenile literature. 2. Popular
culture—Marketing—Juvenile literature. I. Title.
  HF5415.32.W58 2012
  658.8'342—dc23                    2011038005


Visit Compass Point Books on the Internet at www.capstonepub.com

Printed in the United States of America in Stevens Point, Wisconsin.
102011     006404WZS12

# CONTENTS

## CHAPTER 1

# THE MAKINGS OF POP CULTURE

> "Yeah, I'm 16 and I thought that you'd be mine / I used to tweet you and text you and call you and hit you on Facebook all the time ... Can't believe that you did me wrong / We were on iChat all night long."
>
> —Justin Bieber in "Baby"

You make choices every day: what to wear, what to eat, what to watch on TV, and what to listen to on your iPod. Your tastes may be influenced by your parents, your friends, or the other kids at school. You might be trying to fit in. Or you might be trying to stand out. Maybe you are trying to be more like someone you admire, such as a movie star. Maybe you are trying to start your own trend.

Whatever your choices, chances are you're not making them in a vacuum. Whether you realize it or not, you are constantly exposed to advertising. On your way to school, you might see billboards on the side of the road, posters in store windows, and ads on the sides of buses. In the hallways at school, kids wear the logos of their preferred brands or the names of their favorite music groups. If you turn on the TV or the radio, you will see or hear commercials that are targeted at you. On the Internet you are bombarded with banner ads and links to products. The rise of other mobile devices has meant even more exposure to advertising.

Advertising and marketing messages have become more pervasive and more effective over the years. People are exposed to tens of thousands of commercials per year. They might also see thousands of brand names or logos per day. Advertisers have stepped up their efforts to target younger audiences. They know that young people have money to spend. They are trying their hardest to persuade you to spend it on their products.

**Websites often have advertisements called banners on the sides or top of a page. The ads help pay for the costs of the website.**

With so much information being thrown at you, you need to be aware of the intentions behind it. If you can spot the ways marketers are trying to influence you, you can take a more active role in choosing what to give your time and money to. It is important to learn about the forces that drive popular culture and how to recognize and interpret the messages coming at you from all sides. Then you'll be prepared to make your own informed choices.

# COLLEGE-BOUND CONSUMER PROFILE

The National Association of College Stores and Teenage Research Unlimited teamed up to develop a consumer profile for college-bound high school seniors.

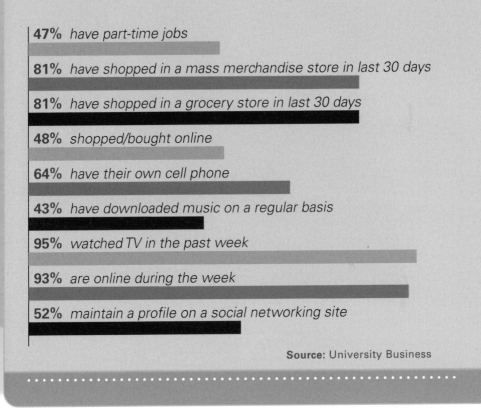

**47%** have part-time jobs

**81%** have shopped in a mass merchandise store in last 30 days

**81%** have shopped in a grocery store in last 30 days

**48%** shopped/bought online

**64%** have their own cell phone

**43%** have downloaded music on a regular basis

**95%** watched TV in the past week

**93%** are online during the week

**52%** maintain a profile on a social networking site

**Source:** University Business

## A Pop Culture Icon

In 2007 Justin Bieber was just a 13-year-old kid in Canada who posted homemade music videos on YouTube. He wanted to share them with his friends

**Justin Bieber's film *Never Say Never* made nearly $30 million in its opening weekend.**

and family members. By July 2008 Bieber was on his way to becoming a sensation. He became the first solo artist to have four singles in the *Billboard* Top 40 before his first album was released. As of 2011 his music video of "Baby" had received more than 500 million views on YouTube. It also held the honors for both most-discussed and most-viewed video. Millions of screaming fans have attended Bieber's concerts and lined up to see his movie, *Never Say Never*.

With his rise to fame, Bieber and his music became part of popular culture. Pop culture, as it is commonly called, includes aspects of culture that are widely known or appeal to a large number of people across a society. It includes TV shows, music and music videos, movies, magazines, and other forms of entertainment and products enjoyed by the mainstream public.

Some people see pop culture as the opposite of high culture. As these people view it, high culture refers to high-quality examples of art and entertainment that are appreciated by a smaller number of people. In contrast, they see pop culture as including things of lower quality or value that have wider appeal. Many people disagree with this description. They do not see a link between quality and popularity.

> Pop culture, as it is commonly called, includes aspects of culture that are widely known or appeal to a large number of people across a society.

# MOVIE OR INFOMERCIAL?

In *Never Say Never*, Justin Bieber plays himself. The movie portrays his success as something resulting from his sheer talent and the devotion of his first fans. Many of these fans like knowing that he's not just another prepackaged product of the major music studios, but rather a kid like them who was found and promoted by other kids. The trailer includes the words: "They said it would never happen. They said he would never make it. But you never stopped believing. The inspiring true story of an ordinary kid you discovered."

Critics have argued that even if Bieber didn't start out as a creation of the mass-produced music industry, he has joined that culture now. "The packagers have certainly arrived," wrote David Edelstein in a movie review for *New York Magazine*. He describes the movie as a brilliant marketing tool. It uses Bieber's modest background and inspiring story to sell him as a product. "This sensationally engineered promo film makes Justin Bieber look like a true force of nature."

Pop culture is also sometimes called mass culture. It refers to products or forms of entertainment that are mass-produced for widespread use for the purposes of making money. In this view, what is popular is largely influenced by what is being heavily promoted.

*Pop culture is also sometimes called mass culture.*

Some people who consider themselves outside the mainstream purposely seek out alternatives to pop culture for this reason.

## Who Decides What's Popular?

You and your friends probably see yourselves as the decision-makers in your own lives. You have your own taste in clothes, you choose the movies you want to see, and you decide which songs to download from iTunes. You have developed your own tastes and your own ideas about what is cool. What you might not have considered is how those tastes have developed. Who or what influences your decisions on what to buy, watch, or listen to?

Whether or not you are thinking about these questions, someone else is. Companies devote large amounts of time, energy, and money to figuring out what will be the next big hit and then promoting it. Pop stars such as Hilary Duff and Miley Cyrus got their starts because a big company—in their case, Disney—selected them to star in their own shows.

Duff started her career as the star of *Lizzie McGuire*. Cyrus played the title role in the Disney Channel series *Hannah Montana*. Both were able to launch successful acting and music careers based on their fame from these shows.

*Large media companies have become more influential in recent decades.*

Large media companies have become more influential in recent decades. In the past companies were limited to owning no more than 28 radio stations. In the mid-20th century radio DJs at local stations chose what songs to play. That meant people heard a variety of music depending on where they lived. If you traveled from one place to another, you might hear a completely different set of songs.

Today that is not the case. In 1996 a new law allowed companies to own an unlimited number of stations. As a result, a small number of large media corporations took ownership of most radio stations in the United States. Clear Channel Communications, for example, controls approximately 1,100 stations. Viacom is another large media company that controls many radio and TV stations. Programming decisions are made at these companies' headquarters. This usually means

At one time DJs got to choose what music was played on a radio station. Now those decisions are primarily made by large media companies based on what the companies think will be most profitable.

that a small number of selections are played on radio stations throughout the country.

The main goal of entertainment companies is to make money. They decide what movies to make, recording artists to promote, or TV shows to produce based on how well they think each will sell. They often make such predictions based on what has sold well in the past. Music labels, for example, need their artists to be played on a large number of radio stations to make money. They focus on artists who have a good chance of appealing to large media owners such as Clear Channel and Viacom.

If a certain kind of music group or singer is popular, media companies start looking for similar performers. This is not a new practice. Back in 1966 the Monkees were launched in response to the success of the Beatles. More recently artists such as Usher, Lil Wayne, and Beyoncé have made hip-hop/R&B a much greater part of popular music. They have paved the way for many similar artists. Sometimes this practice leads to products that seem unoriginal.

Movie studios are another example of an entertainment industry that often sticks to a proven  formula. The *Spider-Man* movie that was made in 2002 grossed more than $820 million worldwide. Other movie studios wanted to copy this success. They've produced a large number of superhero movies in the years since. These movies are often the kinds of blockbuster successes that you are likely to see in major cinema chains, such as AMC or Regal.

Some consumers have turned away from mass-produced entertainment. Many have gone in search of more original work elsewhere. These consumers might listen to a radio station run by a local college, make their own playlists from downloaded songs, or use a free Internet radio service such as Pandora that lets users customize what they hear. Independent movies can be accessed through local art cinemas and have become more available in recent years through rental services such as Netflix.

*Some consumers have turned away from mass-produced entertainment.*

## Media and Culture

A positive movie review, a cover story in a magazine, or a feature on an entertainment news show can boost someone's career or status. A wide array of entertainment-related websites also promote various aspects of popular culture. Conventional news outlets, such as newspapers or magazines, devote sections of their coverage to the latest celebrity news and entertainment reviews. Many bloggers also affect pop culture by posting news, reviews, and recaps. Fan sites, message boards, and social networking sites, such as Facebook, provide even more ways for consumers to stay on top of trends.

The Internet has created new ways for people to break into the entertainment business. Amateur musicians, actors, comedians, or performers can create a website or share their work through sites such as YouTube, MySpace, or Facebook. The Internet has given consumers more choices and more power in determining who will be successful.

*The Internet has given consumers more choices and more power in determining who will be successful.*

Sometimes an indie band or an independent movie will be so good that it will gain buzz—people start talking about it. The 2004 coming-of-age comedy *Napoleon Dynamite* was made for just $400,000. Critics and award show judges didn't like it, but audiences did. It made more than $46 million.

In 2006 the movie *Little Miss Sunshine* told the story of a girl who took a road trip with her unusual family to a beauty pageant. A small studio produced it with an $8 million budget. It premiered at the Sundance Film Festival and received such a positive reaction that it ended up making more than

**The independent movie *Little Miss Sunshine* won Academy Awards for best original screenplay and best supporting actor.** . . . . . . . . . . . . . . . . . . . . . . . . . . . . . . . . . . . . . . . . . . . . . . . . . . . . . . . . . . . . . . . . . . . . . . . . . . . . . .

$100 million. It was nominated for four Academy Awards including best picture.

Justin Bieber is also an example of buzz leading to fame. His homemade videos received thousands of hits on YouTube, and he developed an Internet following. Record executive Scott "Scooter" Braun discovered the videos and started looking for a label to sign Bieber. At first he was met with

Although YouTube can be great for promotion, it doesn't always work that way. In 2011 singer Rebecca Black became a pop culture phenomenon with her music video for her song "Friday." In March 2011 the video went from a few thousand views on YouTube to 6 million hits in less than one week.

However, the attention Black received was mostly negative. Comments on YouTube mocked her voice, her appearance, and the lyrics of the song. It was clear that Black's success was more about how much people disliked the song, rather than liked it.

Even though most of the attention was negative, it catapulted Black into the entertainment scene. Black played a role in Katy Perry's music video for "Last Friday Night." In July 2011 Black released a new single, "My Moment." Although some fans supported Black, critics did not like the new song either.

reluctance from music company executives. They thought Bieber was talented but couldn't succeed without the backing of a major brand such as Nickelodeon or Disney. With the help of the recording artist Usher, Bieber was able to sign a recording contract.

**Although Rebecca Black received mostly negative attention for her YouTube video, she still gained fame and became a pop culture icon.**

What role do you think large companies play in your own entertainment preferences? What other factors influence what you spend your time or money on? In what ways could you take a more active role in these decisions?

## CHAPTER 2

# ADVERTISING'S INFLUENCE

"Sellers catch more prey by blurring the boundaries between advertising and not-advertising. Product placement, viral marketing, and friend-to-friend shilling is all part of the new form—a being that has reduced itself to a single cell that permeates the air you breathe, the sounds around you, the classrooms you endure, and the movies you watch. It's a fully ingrained part of the fabric of life."

—*Carrie McLaren,* Ad Nauseum: A Survivor's Guide to Consumer Culture

Intertwined with pop culture is the world of advertising—anything that is used to promote a product or persuade someone to buy something. Movie studios, record companies, and other members of the entertainment industry all take steps to market their products. Actors promote themselves by appearing on late-night talk

shows. Musicians tour around the world to promote their latest albums.

Consumers of entertainment culture are also bombarded with advertisements for other products. Some are as obvious as a commercial for fruit snacks during a cartoon or a banner ad for the Jonas Brothers' line of watches on the group's official website. Other advertising messages are harder to spot. A company might pay a movie studio to have a character use its product in a movie scene. Some companies ask celebrities to wear their clothes or shoes, hoping that others will copy the celebrities.

## History of Advertising

Word-of-mouth advertising has been around forever, but the first print ads began appearing in newspapers by the 1700s. The first advertising

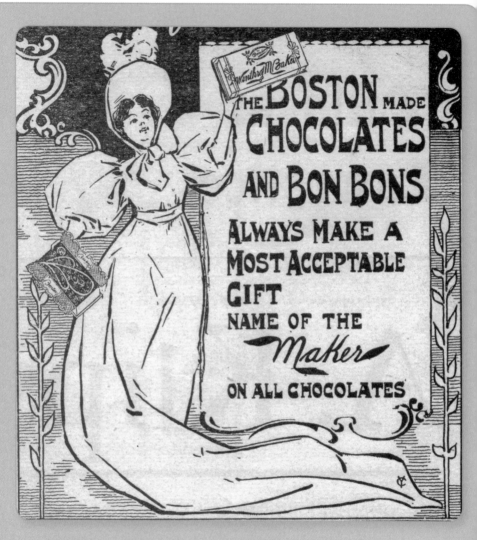

**A 1900 advertisement for chocolates** · · · · · · · · · · · · · · · · · · ·

agencies appeared in the 1800s to sell newspaper space to companies. By the 1920s full-service advertising agencies were developing marketing messages and running large media campaigns.

Early advertising techniques were different from the ones used today. The first print ads were very text heavy. In the late 1800s and early 1900s, print ads tended to have a friendly tone and often covered a product in great detail.

However, no laws existed to prevent ads from exaggerating. Ads for medical products sometimes made unfounded claims about what the products could do. They promised miracle cures for minor and severe illnesses, as well as solutions for problems such as obesity, hair loss, or alcoholism. Such advertisements, whether for products actually called snake oil or similar products, are referred to as "snake oil ads." They were common in the late 1800s and early 1900s.

> *Early advertising techniques were different from the ones used today. The first print ads were very text heavy.*

One such ad for Stanley's Snake Oil described it as a "wonderful pain-destroying compound. The strongest and best liniment known for the cure of all pain and lameness." It claimed to cure an entire list of ailments, such as toothache, back pain, animal bites, and sore throat. Despite its name, the oil did not come from snakes. In 1917 the U.S. government analyzed the contents of supposed snake-oil

# Double Reward

{

**1. brilliant screen projection** of your Kodachrome pictures ... finished as color slides without extra charge

**2. gorgeous Kodachrome Prints** made to order ... in the reasonably priced 2X size shown, or in larger sizes

Amateurs suddenly feel like experts when they discover what wonderful *color* pictures they can take with Kodachrome Film in a miniature camera—any "miniature" with f/6.3 lens or better. Added satisfaction: these superb pictures are so easy to take!

### Fine equipment for less money ...

And now Kodak has produced an ultramodern miniature camera with f/4.5 Lumenized lens selling at the remarkably low price of $29.95, including Federal Tax. Ask your dealer to show you the sensational new Kodak Pony 828 Camera. With it—and Kodaslide Projector, Model 1A, at $29.50—you're well equipped to start your Kodachrome career. Also see Kodaslide Table Viewer—projector, screen, and slide changer combined... and other Kodak miniatures and projectors (Master Model illustrated).

**Eastman Kodak Company, Rochester 4, N. Y.**

## It's Kodak for Color

KODACHROME
DAYLIGHT TYPE

**Kodak**

A Kodak ad from 1950 · · · · · · · · · · · · · · · · · · · · · · · · · · · · · · · · · · · · ·

products. They found them to contain ingredients with little or no medical value, such as mineral oil and red pepper.

Today such practices are referred to as false advertising. The Federal Trade Commission (FTC) is the government agency charged with protecting consumers from harmful business practices. The Federal Trade Commission Act does not allow companies to make misleading or false claims about their products. For example, the FTC has filed numerous lawsuits against companies selling and advertising weight-loss products. Many of the ads promise dramatic weight loss without diet or exercise. The FTC does not approve ads before they are run. Just because an ad makes amazing claims, it does not mean the information is true.

By the 1920s advertisers started to focus less on the facts. Instead they targeted the motivations that drive people to buy something. The reasons didn't have to make sense as long as they appealed to a consumer's impulses or fears. Advertisers took advantage of people's desires to fit in or look attractive. A 1941 Listerine ad, for example, warned women that smelly breath could make them bad kissers. Modern ads may look very different from this early model, but many still use similar tactics.

By the 1950s advertisers started to realize that most readers were not going to read 500 words about a bar of soap. Ads started to feature large, colorful images and fewer words. They focused less on the product and more on the person who might buy it. A common tactic was to emphasize the positive ways a product was going to change a person's life. An ad might have featured an image of a race car driver to imply that the product made people as daring or cool as one.

*An ad might have featured an image of a race car driver to imply that the product made people as daring or cool as one.*

In the 1960s advertisers started making funny ads. They aimed at making people feel as if they were in on a joke or part of a better group of people who lived a certain kind of life. This feeling created a positive association with the product.

Today advertisers have become highly skilled at selling to consumers. Marketers have become sneakier as they try to plant ideas in people's heads without those people realizing they're being manipulated.

## Modern Advertising

In recent years marketing has become more pervasive than ever. In a world with so many choices, products and companies are all fighting for your attention. Advertising serves another purpose as well. Selling advertising is one of the major sources of income for newspapers,

# EXPOSURE TO ADVERTISING

Advertising companies must always make sure their money is going to the most effective place. International financial firm Morgan Stanley issued a report in 2009 showing the percentage of ad money spent on a given medium versus the percentage of time consumers actually devote to that medium.

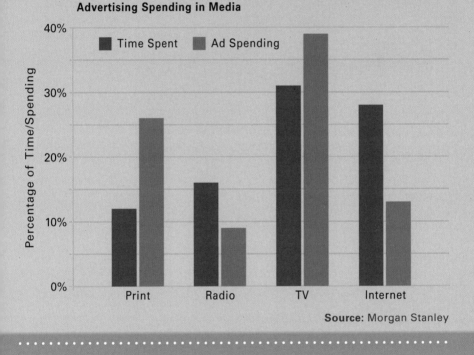

**Advertising Spending in Media**

Percentage of Time/Spending

■ Time Spent  ■ Ad Spending

Print · Radio · TV · Internet

**Source:** Morgan Stanley

magazines, websites, TV stations, and other media outlets. Without it, they would not be able to stay in business.

Some social networking websites can access information from your profile to streamline ads that will interest you. · · · · · · · · · · · · · · · · · · · · · · · · · · · · · · · · · · · · · ·

For decades advertising has been featured in magazines and newspapers, on TV, and on the radio. Even if people don't open the newspaper or turn on the TV, they can hardly leave their homes without seeing ads nearly everywhere—on billboards, signs, and posters. The more kinds of media being used, the more ways advertisers have found to reach consumers. According to the FTC, children between the ages of 2 and 11 view more than 25,000 TV commercials annually. This does not include exposure to other ads and brand names. By some estimates young people see more than 8,000 brands per day.

It's difficult to use the Internet without encountering ads, and not just the obvious banners or pop-up ads. One 8-year-old girl's parents were happy she was spending time on the website for the wholesome Beacon Street Girls book series. But they were disappointed to find that the site contained contests to win free prizes, such as an Ashley Tisdale album or a Little Mermaid prize pack. Such contests are actually a form of advertising—a way to generate interest in the featured products.

*The more kinds of media being used, the more ways advertisers have found to reach consumers.*

## Recommendations from Friends

Advertisers have also started to rely on consumers to spread product messages. If a friend recommends a product or a singer to you, you might be more willing to give it a try than if you heard about it in a TV commercial. The widespread use of electronic communication has made this a more effective marketing strategy. People share what they

People share what they like with their friends through e-mails, instant messages, message boards, texting, or posting on social networking sites.

like with their friends through e-mails, instant messages, message boards, texting, or posting on social networking sites. Through these means an interesting video or website can spread rapidly around the Internet.

In 2004 Burger King created a simple website featuring a video of a person wearing a chicken suit, to promote its new chicken sandwiches. Users of the website type in commands that the chicken then follows. The site has a simple "send to a friend" button. Burger King did not promote the website. It simply relied on people liking the game enough to share it with their friends. To test it out, the designers sent the link to a handful of colleagues, asking for feedback.

This test alone resulted in 1 million hits. In nine months it attracted 385 million visitors. While the game doesn't feature the actual chicken sandwich, it reinforces in its users' heads that Burger King has chicken on the menu. It also creates a positive association with the product.

**Advertisers may show a good-looking model with a product they want you to buy.** · · · · · · · · · · · · · · ·

## Going Viral

When a game, video, or other piece of content spreads rapidly around the Internet, it is referred to as "going viral." Many marketers are trying to create such promotions because they are low-cost and can be very effective. Marketers just have to create something that is fun or interesting enough that people will share it with their friends. The key for consumers is recognizing that while fun, viral content also serves a purpose.

You can enjoy a video or game while still thinking critically about whether it is advertising

When a video online is funny or interesting people want to share it with their friends. · · · · · · · · · · · · · · · · · · · · ·

something of real value to you. If you are wondering whether something you like was created for marketing purposes, look for some of these telltale signs: a prominently featured brand or logo, people who look like models, or a link to a professional-looking website. Here are a few examples of successful viral campaigns:

- In 2010 Old Spice asked people to submit questions for their spokesman. The Old Spice

Guy then made a series of funny videos responding to the questions and referring to the askers by name. The videos were cheap to make and popular because of their entertainment value and personal touch.

- One aspect of the marketing campaign for the website Taxbrain.com was to advertise on the side of a NASCAR race car. The company decided to get more mileage out of this exposure by staging the fake theft of the race car by a crazed fan. The video appeared on YouTube, as well as in other media coverage.

- In 2008 Levi's uploaded a video of guys performing stunts such as backflips and headstands while putting on their jeans. Through sharing and media coverage, the video was seen by more than 100 million people.

Have you ever forwarded a link, video, or game that was created by an advertiser? Why did you do it? Did how much you enjoyed an ad influence whether you would be willing to try the product? Is this a valid reason to make a purchasing choice? What other factors could you consider to make a more informed decision?

# HOW ADVERTISING WORKS

> *"They say TV is free, but we pay for it every time we hum a jingle."*
>
> —*Jason Love, comedian*

Not only have advertising messages become more common, they have also become more effective and more subtle. Instead of directly convincing you to buy a product, many marketers use the power of suggestion. They try to plant a seed in your head without you knowing it. Being aware of the way that advertisers try to influence consumers helps you to remain an independent thinker.

## Tools of Persuasion

Ads use a number of techniques to persuade people to buy or use products. Some techniques are more easily spotted than others. Sometimes ads will simply contain information about the product, what it does, or how it works. Price, including sales or clearances, is another piece of information an ad might relay. Ads might mention a special ingredient or include testimonials—positive reviews by people who have tried the product. Ads often contain positive adjectives such as "amazing" or "incredible" to build hype around the product.

The ad may include a call to action, such as "buy now" or "try this today." It may come in the form of a slogan, such as Nike's "Just do it." Ad slogans have become more subtle over the years. A slogan might reflect a feeling or quality its creators want you to think about in connection with the product. McDonald's uses the recognizable slogan "I'm lovin' it," while Coca-Cola is known for its slogan "It's the real thing." Taco Bell paints itself as a standout with "Think outside the bun." Other slogans are simply catchy, such as "cuckoo for Cocoa Puffs."

**Coca-Cola was invented in 1886 by pharmacist and chemist John Stith Pemberton. It was originally sold for 5 cents a glass. The Coca-Cola Company now operates in more than 200 countries.** · · · · · · · · · · · · · · · · · · ·

Many marketing techniques appeal to emotions. Some ads use the power of association by linking their product with something that is viewed positively. This could be a popular celebrity, an attractive model, or a pleasant image. The ad may try to suggest that you need to have a certain product in order to be happy, successful, popular, or some other desired characteristic.

Other ads may prey on your fears or insecurities about problems such as obesity, acne, bad breath, or being uncool. The commercials for Proactiv acne products employ several of these techniques. In one ad pop artist Katy Perry says, "I love being a free spirit onstage and off. But when you suffer from acne blemishes, you don't feel very free." This pitch combines common insecurities of teenagers about their appearances with the comfort that even celebrities, such as Perry, are in the same boat.

Other ads aim to be memorable. If you remember the ad, you may remember the product. Humor is often an effective way to do this. Many people remember the E-Trade baby who talks like an adult, for example. Other companies may integrate games, activities, prizes, or gifts to draw you in and give their ad lasting impact.

> *Other ads may prey on your fears or insecurities about problems such as obesity, acne, bad breath, or being uncool.*

## Appealing to the Senses

Advertisers try to appeal to as many of the senses as possible so their ads stick in your brain. A fast-food commercial will show a close-up image of a burger so juicy you can almost smell it. Food shown in ads usually has been treated in some way to make it look more appetizing. Food stylists may use oil to make something shinier, paint to make it a

The "Got Milk?" ad campaign uses food stylists to make sure celebrities, including supermodel and TV star Heidi Klum, have perfect milk mustaches.

more appealing color, and toothpicks, cardboard, or hairspray to help hold its shape. The actual product will hardly resemble what was shown in the ad. A food stylist described her job:"I always say my job is to get the customer to buy the product just once—to make them feel like eating. If the food tastes revolting, then that's the manufacturer's problem. Anything is possible—if you have the time. If I was doing a commercial burger shoot, I would ask for around 400 buns and go through them all to find the perfect specimen."

Sound is another powerful tool. A car commercial might incorporate trendy or catchy music that you'll be humming later. Sometimes a simple sound effect or short jingle is effective. In 1939 Pepsi became one of the first big companies to advertise its product with a jingle. Today many people can hum the three-note Intel sound, Subway's $5 Footlong song, or Chili's baby back ribs jingle.

Advertisers pay to use popular songs in commercials, hoping to catch the attention of fans of a particular kind of music. Sprite uses hip-hop music in its ads to try to make its product appealing to fans. Some artists will license their music. Companies have paid such stars as Britney Spears,

*Companies have paid such stars as Britney Spears, Madonna, and Moby to use their music for marketing purposes.*

Madonna, and Moby to use their music for marketing purposes. Moby explained his decision by pointing out that the deal meant more people would hear his music. Other artists admit to doing it for the money. Making money through ads can be particularly important for indie music groups that do not earn much money from sales or tours. Hamilton Leithauser of the indie rock band The Walkmen said making money was the primary reason the group licensed its music for a Saturn car commercial. "Selling songs to advertisers was a way for us as an independent band to make extra money and spend time concentrating on music and not have to work at another job," Leithauser explained. Other performers view this practice as selling out and do not let their music be used in this way. R.E.M. and Bruce Springsteen have turned down offers to license their songs.

## Interactive Ads

Online games make it possible to engage more of your senses than ever before. These games create constant interaction with a consumer. Honey Nut

**The McDonald's sign is probably the most recognized fast food symbol around the world.** · · · · · · · · · · ·

Cheerios has a Create a Comic game that lets users drag artwork and phrases onto a page to create their own comic strips featuring the Cheerios honeybee. Some special effects and artwork can only be accessed using a special code from the cereal box. Games promote other sugary cereals such as Fruity Pebbles, Apple Jacks, and Lucky Charms. McDonald's is another company that has an online gaming presence. At the McWorld website, kids can create a character and use it to visit fun places, play games, and do other activities. Codes from Happy Meal products are needed to unlock some of the

# COLOR IN ADVERTISING

Advertisers use colors to trigger various responses in the brain.

- Red can correlate to passion, love, energy, or danger. It might be used in an ad for lipstick.
- Orange suggests warmth or happiness. It's a popular choice for food or toy ads.
- Yellow is another cheerful color. Advertisers sometimes avoid it because it suggests childishness or instability.
- Green is associated with nature and safety. It is often used in ads for medicines.
- Blue represents calmness, stability, and cleanliness. It is good for promoting household cleaners.
- Purple combines energy with stability. It is also associated with wealth or royalty.
- White suggests purity and cleanliness. It's used to advertise medical products, charities, and cleaners.
- Black sometimes carries a negative connotation, but it also can signify mystery or glamour. Sometimes it is used to suggest sophistication.

features. The McWorld site has a banner at the top that reads, "Hey kids! This is advertising." This is the company's attempt to be open about the purpose of the site.

These ads work not only by encouraging brand recognition, but also by creating another reason to buy the product—to obtain the special codes. Such games are also shared between friends through social networking sites so that the ads reach even more people. Popular online game sites such as McWorld receive hundreds of thousands of visits each month.

> *These ads work not only by encouraging brand recognition, but also by creating another reason to buy the product— to obtain the special codes.*

What advertising techniques do you think are most effective and why? How conscious are you of the various ways an ad is trying to persuade you? What makes an ad memorable to you? Have you played an online game related to a product? Have you shared such a game with a friend? How did the game affect your relationship with that product?

## CHAPTER 4

# TARGETED MESSAGES

"Almost every aspect of today's tween-ager is different from what we have seen among past generations. They've grown up faster, are more connected, more direct and more informed. They have more personal power, more money, influence and attention than any generation before them."

—*Martin Lindstrom,* Brand Child

To have maximum impact, most ads are directed at a specific group of people. This target audience might be teenagers, working mothers, seniors, or men between the ages of 18 and 35. Advertisers base the content of the ad on what will be most persuasive to the target audience. They also decide when or where to place an ad to have the best chance of reaching the group most likely to buy or use the product.

In recent years advertisers have stepped up their efforts to reach children and teens.

Tweens—children between the ages of 8 and 12—are a growing demographic. The U.S. Census Bureau has projected there will be 23 million tweens by 2020. Marketers are particularly interested in reaching this group for several reasons. Many tweens have disposable income from gifts, allowances, and odd jobs. Tweens spend approximately $50 billion of their own money annually.

In addition to making their own buying decisions, tweens influence how their parents or other family members spend money. Young people can be persistent and convincing. One survey found that six out of 10 children will keep asking their parents for something they want, even after their parents say no, an average of nine times. One marketing expert calls this influence "pester power." He estimated $188 billion is spent each year because of children directly influencing their parents.

**Many young girls' buying decisions are motivated by a desire to fit in. Many clothing brands specifically target girls and young women for this reason.**

Advertisers also see tweens as a group that might be more easily persuaded than older consumers. Many tweens are highly brand-conscious. They desire to fit in and have insecurities typical of their age group. "Though tweens are old enough to be seduced by advertising, they're too young to spot its tricks—promises of popularity, plays on their fears of [exclusion], identification with stars," wrote journalist Jeffrey Kluger.

## Brand Loyalty

While tastes change often during tween years, companies are hoping to make lasting customers. Children begin to recognize logos and brand names from a very young age, according to research. This is why children's and teen's versions of magazines such as *Time*, *Sports Illustrated*, and *People* all carry ads for adult products. The hope is that repeated exposure to the brand name will turn kids into future customers.

> *While tastes change often during tween years, companies are hoping to make lasting customers.*

When a person continues to buy a certain brand over an extended time, it is called brand loyalty. Companies want to create lasting bonds with young customers. Peer pressure is an obstacle because children tend to be more influenced by their peers than by loyalty to a brand. But some brands, such as McDonald's and Adidas, have managed to have staying power.

## Product Placement

Viewing full-length commercials may quickly be becoming a thing of the past. Devices such as DVRs allow people to record their favorite shows and then fast forward through commercials. Online video services such as Netflix and Hulu minimize the number of commercials too. Advertisers have had to become sneakier in reaching people.

When a company pays to have its product appear in a movie, TV show, or video game, it is called product placement. If you see a character drink a particular brand of soda or drive a certain make of car, chances are that the company paid big bucks for its product to be included. Seeing the product creates brand recognition and possibly a positive association. Product placement has a history of being effective. For example, Reese's Pieces gained popularity after it was shown as the favorite food of E.T. in the 1982 movie. Today hit shows such as *American Idol* and *Celebrity Apprentice* feature hundreds, even thousands, of product placements per season. They range from beverages to clothing choices.

*When a company pays to have its product appear in a movie, TV show, or video game, it is called product placement.*

Product placement has also started to show up in the world of video games. Some games are brands themselves. They promote a franchised character

# THE OPPOSITE OF PRODUCT PLACEMENT—OR IS IT?

Sometimes a company or brand might not want to be associated with a certain character or celebrity. A company might ask for its logo to be blurred or removed from a shot if it feels the association with a negative character might hurt the image of its product. In 2011 retail company Abercrombie & Fitch offered to pay cast members of the *Jersey Shore*, a popular MTV reality show, not to wear its brand on TV. Abercrombie & Fitch issued a statement claiming that the association of one particular cast member, Mike "the Situation" Sorrentino, with its clothing was damaging the reputation of the brand. Some product placement experts said the offer was actually a publicity stunt designed to bring more publicity to both the brand and the show. They argued that by issuing such a statement, Abercrombie & Fitch was actually drawing more attention to the fact that *Jersey Shore* cast members wore its clothing. What do you think?

such as James Bond or Spider-Man. The characters help sell the game because they are already popular. They also serve as advertising for the rest of the franchise, which may include movies, toys, clothing, and more. Sometimes a product will appear within

A makeup artist uses Covergirl mascara on
*America's Next Top Model* winner Eva Pigford
on the show. The reality show's winners become
spokespeople for Covergirl.

a game. A player might drive a certain kind of car
or use a particular brand of cell phone in the course
of the game. A brand name might also appear in the

# TOP 10 BRANDS WITH PRODUCT PLACEMENT

Some brands use product placement as an advertising technique more than others. A study by the Nielsen Company counted the number of times a product was shown during prime-time broadcasts from March 1 to March 31, 2011.

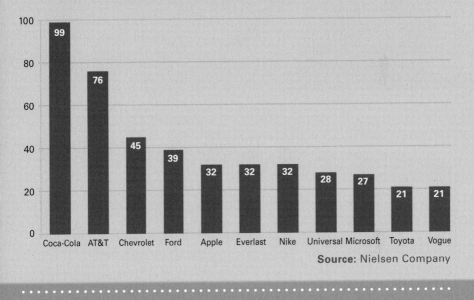

| | | |
|---|---|---|
| Coca-Cola | 99 | |
| AT&T | 76 | |
| Chevrolet | 45 | |
| Ford | 39 | |
| Apple | 32 | |
| Everlast | 32 | |
| Nike | 32 | |
| Universal | 28 | |
| Microsoft | 27 | |
| Toyota | 21 | |
| Vogue | 21 | |

**Source:** Nielsen Company

scenery, such as on a vending machine. These kinds of placements occur with or without payment.

Some marketers think that today's kids have become smarter about recognizing product placements. As a result advertisers have found other ways to reach children. Some companies

**Brazilian surfer Adriano de Souza competes in the Billabong Rio Pro men's surfing competition in Brazil. Souza won the competition in 2011.**

stage events, such as the Billabong surfing contests or Adidas basketball competitions. They create online games, activities, and videos to be enjoyed and shared.

Many companies use Facebook and other social networking sites to advertise products. Once you "like" a product, you receive updates and offers in your Facebook feed. Internet users also share links to videos or other advertising content through Facebook, e-mail, texting, and message boards. These sharing methods effectively turn users into marketers.

## Limits on Advertising to Children

The FTC has a history of regulating ads targeted at children to shield them from false claims or protect them from harm. It has brought a number of false advertising lawsuits against advertisers for using special effects to show toys doing things that they could not do in real life. In such cases FTC officials consider the ad from the point of view of a child who would be viewing it.

*Many companies use Facebook and other social networking sites to advertise products.*

For example, a toy helicopter might be shown flying when it is really suspended by wires. While an adult might recognize that the toy helicopter did not really fly, a young child would expect it to work as shown.

The FTC has also challenged ads that make questionable claims about the nutritional value of foods aimed at children. Wonder Bread, for instance, had to stop running commercials that claimed its bread helped improve memory and brain function. In other cases the FTC has looked out for the safety

Channel One is a 12-minute news broadcast that is shown to students in more than 8,000 middle and high schools. It is offered free to schools. Many schools use the broadcast to teach students about current events. However, Channel One includes two minutes of commercials in order to pay for itself. According to the Channel One website, the company is careful to keep advertising appropriate to show children.

Critics have objected to commercials in material that is meant to be educational. While researching children's reactions to advertising, educator Roy Fox talked to more than 200 children about commercials they saw on Channel One. He found many children misunderstood the purpose of these ads. When asked why a basketball player would appear in an ad for Nike shoes, some kids thought the commercial motivated the player to play better or helped his team. Others thought the player got to appear in the commercial as a reward for hard work. "Talking further with these students, I realized they did not realize that commercials were designed to sell products or services," Fox wrote.

of children. For example, a discontinued Uncle Ben's Rice commercial showed a young child using a stove without supervision.

**A study conducted on Nike ads showed that many children do not realize that the purpose of commercials is to sell a product.** . . . . . . . . . . . . . . . . . . . . . . . . . . . . . .

The Children's Television Act of 1990 restricts the amount of commercial time during children's shows. A single hour of children's TV programming can contain 10.5 minutes of commercials on weekends and 12 minutes on weekdays. This does not apply to other programming that children view. It also does not lessen the amount of advertising that children see elsewhere.

**The Federal Communications Commission limits commercials in children's programming.**

Some critics are particularly concerned about children's exposure to online ads and games. Groups such as Campaign for Commercial-Free Childhood and Media Awareness Network have tried to inform people of this issue. "Food marketers have tried to reach children since the age of the carnival barker, but they've never had so much access to them and never been able to bypass parents so successfully," said Susan Linn, director of Campaign for Commercial-Free Childhood.

Some industry leaders argue that companies have been more careful about how they market to children in recent years. Some large companies have signed a pledge with the Children's Food and Beverage Advertising Initiative, associated with the Better Business Bureau. In the pledge they agree to avoid product placement in children's movies. They also promise to include more healthful products in interactive games, among other things. General Mills, McDonald's, Pepsi, and Coca-Cola have signed the pledge.

*Some critics are particularly concerned about children's exposure to online ads and games.*

Representatives of the Children's Food and Beverage Advertising Initiative have said companies that have signed the pledge have complied with it. They have shut down several online game sites that advertised to children. Critics, on the other hand, say

Many companies have agreed not to incorporate product placement into programs geared specifically toward children. But these companies still incorporate their products into family shows such as *American Idol*.

that the pledge is filled with loopholes. They say it fails to define which products and advertising methods are suitable for children.

Some people think children need to be protected from advertising because they are too vulnerable to its messages. Do you feel this is an accurate thing to say about you or your peers? Do you

# TOP FIVE SHOWS WITH PRODUCT PLACEMENT

Some TV shows allow product placement more than others. *American Idol* is well known for having a lot of product placement.

The Nielsen Company counted the occurrences of product placement in several popular shows from March 1 to March 31, 2011.

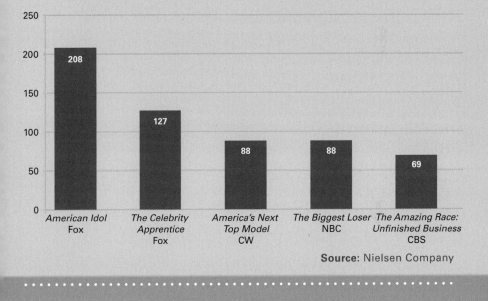

| | |
|---|---|
| 208 | American Idol — Fox |
| 127 | The Celebrity Apprentice — Fox |
| 88 | America's Next Top Model — CW |
| 88 | The Biggest Loser — NBC |
| 69 | The Amazing Race: Unfinished Business — CBS |

**Source:** Nielsen Company

think limits need to be placed on advertising to children, tweens, and teens? Why or why not? What else could be done to lessen advertising's impact on children?

## CHAPTER 5

# THE POWER OF CELEBRITY

*"If you look at sport and entertainment, coverage used to be about the sport, or the entertainment. Now it's all about personalities, which makes endorsement all the more effective."*

—Matthew Patten, founder of international advertising agency M&C Saatchi Sponsorship

For as long as music and TV have been around, celebrities have influenced the rest of us. Half a century before Justin Bieber turned masses of fans into "Beliebers," the Beatles were igniting Beatlemania. Men started wearing the Beatles' tailored suits and pointed boots.

Musicians tried to copy the group's new rock sound. In the 1950s James Dean popularized sideburns and a rebellious attitude. In the 1980s Madonna pioneered the "material girl" persona. She inspired young girls to wear lacy and flesh-baring clothes. Trends such as these

spread nationally, and even globally, as millions of teens tried to copy their idols.

Modern technology has only increased the presence of celebrities in our lives. We not only see them at the movie theater, but we are also bombarded with their images in magazines, on gossip blogs, and in 24-hour news reports. Information about what famous people are doing spreads quickly through texting and social media. But new technology also means a greater variety of choices. "In today's world, this lofty power no longer belongs to a handful of celebrities," wrote marketing expert Martin Lindstrom in *Brand Child*. "The instant communication across the globe between tweens has made it possible for the entire generation to adopt and develop certain trends and keep them alive for months."

Madonna has been an international pop star
since her start in 1984.

## Celebrity Endorsements

For years celebrities have been making extra
money by doing endorsements for products.
Companies pay actors, athletes, or other well-known

figures to appear in TV commercials, magazine ads, or other advertising materials. Basketball player Michael Jordan, for example, has been a spokesman for Nike, Wheaties, McDonald's, Gatorade, Hanes, and MCI. In 2010 tennis player Maria Sharapova signed an eight-year deal to advertise for Nike. She would reportedly earn $70 million from Nike.

Recognizing a celebrity gets viewers' attention. Fans of the celebrity might develop a positive association with the products. Celebrities may claim they have benefited from the products or simply let their images be associated with the products. Companies want consumers to associate their products with being attractive, successful, and cool.

*Companies pay actors, athletes, or other well-known figures to appear in TV commercials, magazine ads, or other advertising materials.*

Makeup companies often hire celebrities to imply that they use the products to help them look beautiful. For example, spokeswomen for Revlon have included actresses Jessica Alba, Halle Berry, and Jessica Biel. Other marketing campaigns are more creative in how they incorporate big names. In 2011 Justin Bieber and Ozzy Osbourne appeared in a Super Bowl commercial for Best Buy that captured viewers' attention with humor. The commercial made fun of Osbourne for being out of touch, while Osbourne poked fun at Bieber's hair. The commercial got a lot of attention for being clever and hip.

Some celebrities also make money by selling their own products. The Jonas Brothers have a line of watches. Miley Cyrus joined with fashion designer Max Azria to start her own clothing line. Hip-hop artists Jay-Z and 50 Cent have also made millions of dollars from personal clothing lines. In such cases consumers have to be careful that they are purchasing products they genuinely like and not just buying things because they like the celebrity.

## A More Subtle Approach

While it's usually easy to tell when a celebrity spokesperson was hired to sell a product, sometimes celebrities help sell goods in less obvious ways. Companies often gain exposure by paying celebrities to use or wear their goods. A fashion designer sends free clothing to a famous actress hoping she will wear it. When she wears the clothing to an event, photographers take pictures. These pictures appear on Internet sites or in fashion

**Celebrities can be just as successful at marketing their own or other companies' products as the talent they are famous for. Hip-hop artist Jay-Z has made millions off his clothing line.** . . . . . . . . . . . . . . . . . . . . . . . . . . . . . . . . . . . .

magazines. People who are interested in fashion—or the actress—try to copy the look.

This strategy isn't used only by high fashion brands. Sportswear companies get famous athletes to use or wear their products. The companies want to give the impression that their products help these athletes play as well as they do.

Actor and comedian David Cross wrote about his experience visiting an exclusive Nike store in Los Angeles. As one of its marketing strategies, the company gives free apparel to celebrities. A consultant showed Cross around the store, loading him up with products to take home. Cross donated most of his Nike apparel to Goodwill. But other celebrities wear it and, in doing so, promote the Nike brand.

## Licensed Characters

Companies sometimes create or license characters to sell products. When a character is licensed, its creator is paid by other companies that want to use it. For example, Disney receives money when manufacturers make *Cars* character Lightning McQueen toys or dishes. Licensing is profitable for business. In 2010 Disney made more than $28 billion from its licensing agreements, which included products featuring *Toy Story 3* characters. Warner Bros. made

> *Companies sometimes create or license characters to sell products.*

The Harry Potter franchise is estimated to be worth $21 billion with merchandise, video games, and other commercial tie-in sales. In 2010 Universal Orlando Resort opened The Wizarding World of Harry Potter, a new theme park.

$6 billion that year for licensing Harry Potter and Looney Tunes products.

Because licensing can be so profitable, entertainment companies often plan content with these types of deals in mind. Children's movies and action or superhero movies are often conceived in this way. When the Toy Story franchise was being developed, Disney executives knew a movie about

*When the Toy Story franchise was being developed, Disney executives knew a movie about toys would mean lots of opportunities to make money selling those toys.*

toys would mean lots of opportunities to make money selling those toys. Sequels of popular movies help sell even more toys and products.

TV shows also often have product tie-ins. For instance, if you enjoy *SpongeBob SquarePants*, you might buy a SpongeBob board game. Video games also often have licensing agreements. Pokémon began as a Nintendo video game. It grew to include a massive trading-card industry, as well as cartoons, movies, action figures, and apparel. Some people consider shows such as *Yu-Gi-Oh!* and *Dragon Ball Z* to be full-length advertisements for their associated trading cards.

## Controversial Characters

Joe Camel was a cartoon character known to many kids. The character appeared in magazines, on billboards, and in other print ads from 1987 until 1997 to promote cigarettes. In 1991 the American Medical Association conducted a study to test logo recognition among 3- to 6-year-olds. A group of preschoolers was given a set of logos

# CELEBRITY BACKLASH

Using a celebrity to advertise a product does not always turn out as planned. Because a celebrity is a real person, advertisers cannot predict what he or she might do. When celebrities who have advertised products get bad publicity for something that has happened in their lives, it can affect consumers' opinions about both the celebrity and the product.

For example, in 2009 singer Chris Brown was arrested for assault. Brown had been featured in advertisements for Doublemint gum. But the company suspended the advertisements after Brown's arrest. Because of Brown's actions, the company did not want him connected to their product.

and a set of brands and asked to match them. Thirty percent of 3-year-olds and more than 90 percent of 6-year-olds correctly matched Joe Camel to cigarettes. Previous studies had found a link between cigarette advertising and underage smoking. Many people found this troubling. In 1997 Camel responded to pressure from Congress and the public by discontinuing its use of Joe Camel in its ads.

While Joe Camel is no longer around, the main conclusion of the 1991 study remains relevant—very young children pay attention to advertising messages. The issue has come up again in recent years, as people have debated whether cartoon characters should be used to advertise high-sugar foods marketed to young children. Such characters include the Keebler Elves, Toucan Sam, Ronald McDonald, and Cap'n Crunch. In April of 2011 the FTC and three other agencies proposed new voluntary guidelines that would curb this practice. The guidelines encourage advertisers to either use their colorful characters to advertise healthier choices, or to stop using the characters. The guidelines applied not only to TV and print ads, but also to social media, movie product placement, and online games.

Proponents of stricter guidelines argue that rising obesity rates among children make advertising choices a health issue. The companies involved say they are already making efforts to reduce sugar and add whole grains to their products. In the meantime, many people have pushed to educate

**Ronald McDonald is an easily recognizable character used to market McDonald's fast food restaurants to children. Some question the ethics of marketing unhealthy food with cartoon characters.** · · · · · · · · · · · · · · · · · · · · · · · ·

children about the advertising they are exposed
to. PBS Kids has a website called Don't Buy It
that explores media literacy. The FTC has created

**Once you know how advertising influences you, you will be ready to make informed choices about the things you buy.** · · · · · · · · · · · · · · · · · · · · · · · · · · · · · · · · · ·

an online game called Admongo to educate kids about the world of marketing. The idea behind such programs is to give young people the tools to sort through the advertising directed at them. With a better idea of how and why the messages are being delivered, young consumers can make more informed choices about how to spend their money and time.

Have you or would you purchase a product that a celebrity you admire has used, worn, or endorsed? Why or why not? What factors would you consider when making such a purchase? Is it wrong for companies to market unhealthful foods to children using fun characters? If you think this is a problem, how should it be addressed?

**Here are some exercises that will help you experience media literacy concepts first-hand.**

**1** With a notebook in hand, watch one of your favorite movies and write down all the brand names you see in the movie. They might include foods and beverages, items of clothing, toys, or a car someone is driving. Afterward look at your list and identify which brands are ones that you use or would consider using.

Why do you use or want to use these brands?

Did seeing the brand in the movie affect your opinion of the brand or willingness to buy its products?

**2** Visit Admongo.gov, a website designed by the Federal Trade Commission to educate tweens about advertising. Design a character and use it to explore a special online world while you learn about recognizing marketing messages and making informed buying decisions. You will be asked to identify various kinds of advertisements and to think about what they are trying to get you to do.

**3** Make a list of your five most recent purchases. For each one, consider what influenced you to buy it.

Did your parents, friends, or favorite celebrities affect any of your choices?

Can you remember seeing any advertisements or marketing messages related to any of the products, and do you think they affected your choices?

How much did usefulness, personal taste, or cost determine your choices?

**4** Find half a dozen ads in magazines or newspapers. As you look at them, ask yourself who paid for the ads and what they are trying to sell.

What techniques are they using to persuade you? Remember, this can include information, hype words, calls to action or slogans, celebrity spokespeople, colors, or appeals to your emotions.

How effective do you think each of the ads is?

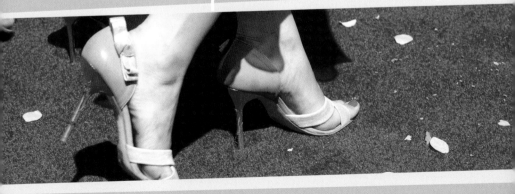

# GLOSSARY

**brand loyalty**
a consumer's long-term commitment to purchasing a product made by a specific company

**consumer**
a person who makes purchases

**consumer profile**
characteristics and behaviors that make up a consumer of a specific product or service

**demographic**
a section of the population with certain characteristics, such as age or gender

**endorsement**
recommendation of a product, often in exchange for money

**franchise**
the right of a company to market products related to a certain brand or character

**hype**
over-the-top promotion of a product

**license**
permission granted by a copyright holder to use content or a character

**logo**
a symbol that represents a company or brand that is designed to be easily recognizable

**mainstream**
a common activity, idea, or preference

**slogan**
a brief attention-getting phrase used in advertising

**testimonial**
an expression of appreciation or gratitude

**viral**
quickly and widely spread through electronic communication

# ADDITIONAL RESOURCES

## Investigate Further

Burstein, John. *Big Fat Lies: Advertising Tricks*. New York: Crabtree Pub., 2008.

Graydon, Shari. *Made You Look: How Advertising Works and Why You Should Know*. Toronto: Annick, 2003.

Hensley, Laura. *Advertising Attack*. Chicago: Raintree, 2011.

## Internet Sites

Use FactHound to find Internet sites related to this book. All of the sites on FactHound have been researched by our staff.

Here's all you do:

Visit *www.facthound.com*

Type in this code: 9780756545185

## Keep Exploring Media Literacy!

Read the other books in this series:

**Choosing News:** *What Gets Reported and Why*

**Selling Ourselves:** *Marketing Body Images*

**Violence as Entertainment:** *Why Aggression Sells*

# SOURCE NOTES

## Chapter 1:

Page 4, opening quote: David Edelstein. "I'm a Belieber." *New York Magazine*. 11 Feb. 2011. 18 April 2011. http://nymag.com/movies/reviews/71669/

Page 7, graph: "A NACS survey shows that teens have a lot of spending power." Stats Watch. University Business. 1 May 2007. 18 Oct. 2011. www.universitybusiness.com/article/stats-watch-5

Page 10, sidebar, line 14: "Justin Bieber: *Never Say Never* Movie Trailer Official." YouTube. 25 Oct. 2010. 18 Oct. 2011. www.youtube.com/watch?v=COJCN3Mhr14

Page 10, sidebar, line 25: David Edelstein. "I'm a Belieber." *The New York Times*. 11 Feb. 2011. 18 Oct. 2011. http://nymag.com/movies/reviews/71669/

## Chapter 2:

Page 20, opening quote: Carrie McLaren and Jason Torchinsky, eds. *Ad Nauseum: A Survivor's Guide to American Consumer Culture*. New York: Faber and Faber, 2009, p. 8.

Page 23, line 20: Joe Nickell. "Peddling Snake Oil." *Skeptical Inquirer*. December 1998. 18 Oct. 2011. www.csicop.org/sb/show/peddling_snake_oil

Page 27, graph: "Media Time Spent vs. Ad Spend Still Out of Whack." *Business Insider*. 2009. 18 Oct. 2011. www.businessinsider.com/mary-meekers-web-2010-11#-15

Page 28, line 8: "Children's Exposure to TV Advertising in 1977 and 2004." Federal Trade Commission Bureau of Economics Staff Report. 1 June 2007. 18 Oct. 2011. www.ftc.gov/os/2007/06/cabecolor.pdf

Page 29, line 2: Martin Lindström. *Brand Child: Remarkable Insights into the Minds of Today's Global Kids and Their Relationships With Brands* London: Kogan Page, 2003, p. 6.

## Chapter 3:

Page 34, opening quote: Terry O'Reilly and Mike Tennant. The *Age of Persuasion: How Marketing Ate Our Culture*. Berkeley, Calif. Counterpoint, 2009, p. 49.

Page 37, line 5: "Katy Perry—Proactiv TV Commercial." YouTube. 17 Feb. 2011. 18 Oct. 2011. www.youtube.com/watch?v=moPZNg-2878

Page 39, line 5: "Tricks of the Trade." *Guardian*. 4 March 2003. 18 Oct. 2011. www.guardian.co.uk/media/2003/mar/05/marketingandpr.advertising

Page 40, line 14: "The Walkmen and Their Car Commercial." PBS Kids Don't Buy It! 18 Oct. 2011. http://pbskids.org/dontbuyit/entertainment/makingmusic_pg4.html

Page 42, line 2: McWorld. 18 Oct. 2011. http://mcworld.happymeal.com/en_US/index.html

## Chapter 4:

Page 44, opening quote: *Brand Child*. p. 1.

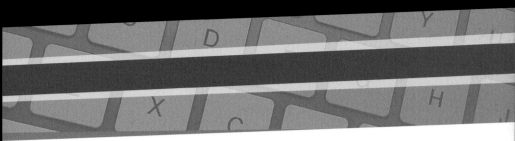

Page 45, line 2: Karyn M. Peterson. "Target: Tweens. Marketers make the most of a diverse demographic of girls." 1 Aug.2009. 18 Oct. 2011. www.giftsanddec.com/article/524091-Target_Tweens.php

Page 45, line 12: *Brand Child: Remarkable Insights into the Minds of Today's Global Kids and Their Relationships With Brands*, p. 47.

Page 45, line 16: Ibid.

Page 46, line 5: Jeffrey Kluger. "How to Hype-proof Your Teen." *Good Housekeeping.* July 2010. 18 Oct. 2011. www.goodhousekeeping.com/family/teens/tween-shopping-peer-pressure-2

Page 51, graph: "Product Placement Hits High Gear on *American Idol,* Broadcast's Top Series for Brand Mentions." AdAge Mediaworks. 18 April 2011. 18 Oct. 2011. http://adage.com/article/mediaworks/product-placement-hits-high-gear-american-idol/227041

Page 54, sidebar, line 34: Sheila Shayon. "Are Advergames Fair Game for Kids?" brandchannel. 2 June 2011. 18 Oct. 2011. www.brandchannel.com/home/post/2011/06/02/Advergames-and-Kids.aspx

Page 57, line 2: *Ad Nauseum: A Survivor's Guide to American Consumer Culture.* p. 128.

Page 59, graph: "Product Placement Hits High Gear on *American Idol,* Broadcast's Top Series for Brand Mentions."

**Chapter 5:**
Page 60, opening quote: Jojo Moyes. "The Naked Truth about Celebrity Endorsements." *The Independent.* 25 Aug. 2000. 18 Oct. 2011. www.independent.co.uk/news/uk/this-britain/the-naked-truth-about-celebrity-endorsements-710729.html

Page 61, line 11: *Brand Child,* pp. 4–5.

Page 66, line 21: Daniel Frankel. "Report: Disney Raked in $28.6B From Licensed Merchandise in 2010." *The Wrap.* 18 May 2011. 18 Oct. 2011. www.thewrap.com/media/article/report-disney-made-286b-2010-licensed-merchandise-27526

# SELECT BIBLIOGRAPHY

Lindström, Martin. *Brand Child: Remarkable Insights into the Minds of Today's Global Kids and Their Relationships With Brands.* London: Kogan Page, 2003.

McLaren, Carrie, and Jason Torchinsky, eds. *Ad Nauseum: A Survivor's Guide to American Consumer Culture.* New York: Faber and Faber, 2009.

Springer, Paul. *Ads to Icons: How Advertising Succeeds in a Multimedia Age.* London: Kogan Page, 2009.

Quart, Allissa. *Branded: The Buying and Selling of Teenagers.* Cambridge, Mass: Perseus, 2003.

# INDEX

## ABOUT THE AUTHOR

Erika Wittekind is a freelance writer and editor based in Wisconsin. She has covered education and government for several community newspapers, winning an award for best local news story from the Minnesota Newspaper Association for 2002.

Harris County Public Library, Houston, TX